# Famous Feet

Look and see if you can tell the story friends you know so well.

### story by Hannah Markley • illustrations by Joe Boddy

**HARCOURT BRACE & COMPANY**

Orlando  Atlanta  Austin  Boston  San Francisco  Chicago  Dallas  New York
Toronto  London

Famous climbing feet.

Famous little cub feet.

Famous running feet.